Cure
Your
Slice
Forever!

Cure Your Slice Forever!

By JOHN HUGGAN,
Golf Digest's Senior Editor of Instruction

Foreword by DAN JENKINS
Illustrated by Dom Lupo

POCKET BOOKS
New York   London   Toronto   Sydney   Tokyo   Singapore

Published by:

NYT SPECIAL SERVICES, INC.
A New York Times Company
5520 Park Avenue, Box 395
Trumbull, CT 06611-0395

and

POCKET BOOKS, a division of Simon & Schuster Inc.
1230 Avenue of the Americas
New York, NY 10020

Illustrations by Dom Lupo

Photography by Stephen Szurlej

Book design by John Newcomb Design Associates

ISBN: 0-671-89235-5

Library of Congress Cataloging-in-Publication Number: 94-65676

First NYT SPECIAL SERVICES, INC. and Pocket Books trade paperback
printing June 1994

10 9 8 7 6 5 4 3 2

POCKET and colophon are registered trademarks
of Simon & Schuster Inc.

GOLF DIGEST/TENNIS, INC. and logos are trademarks of
Golf Digest/Tennis, Inc., A New York Times Company

Printed in the U.S.A.

Contents

Foreword

by Dan Jenkins

Any golfer with a reasonable amount of experience knows that a hook can burn down whole villages while a slice is just a blight on the neighborhood.

I have personal knowledge of this, having dealt for long periods of time with both a chronic hook and a chronic slice.

This, in fact, is why a slice is infinitely more evil and disgusting.

There is nothing manly about a slice, to put it simply.

After all, a hook shows that you know how to hold and swing the golf club. Your swing can actually look *good* when you hit a hook that may still be running long after Niagara Falls has dried up.

But a slice? It's not pretty, in any form. It doesn't *go* anywhere. Sure, it may hang in the air like the Goodyear blimp, but when it comes down it's either on the patio of the condo or unplayable in the ditch or just a few yards past the ladies tee.

A hook can at least give you something angry to say with conviction, like, "That's right–hook some more, bitch!"

But there's nothing to do as you gaze at your slice but sigh again and wonder about the nerd that's inhabited your body.

A hook is a stormy romance, a slice is a pre-nuptial agreement.

A hook is meat and potatoes, a slice is sculpted carrots and Chef Timothy's coconut veal.

A hook is John Wayne, a slice is Liberace.

A hook is a football game, a slice is a croquet tournament.

A hook don't wear a lot of jewelry.

A slice sells software.

If a slice had a line in a movie, it would be, "Love means never having to say you're sorry."

If a hook had a line in a movie, it would be, "Mother of God, is this the end of Rico?"

Okay, you get the point.

Now you have to let John Huggan cure your slice so you will be a happier, more contented golfer, not to mention person.

Actually, I don't think John can help you--he's never hit anything but a long, straight ball. But he knows all these experts, and if there's a cure for the hated slice anywhere in the world, it's in this book.

Read it and hook.

Golf Digest Columnist Dan Jenkins' latest book is <u>You Gotta Play Hurt.</u>

Introduction

No publication is more qualified to cure your slice than Golf Digest. For more than 40 years now the magazine has been fighting the handicap golfer's biggest battle: how to stop that ball curving from left-to-right. During that time the slice has been analyzed from every angle, dissected, taken apart, put back together and rearranged. It hasn't been x-rayed yet, but you get the feeling it's only a matter of time.

And it hasn't been just anyone doing the analyzing. The Golf Digest Instruction Staff reads like a who's-who of teaching and playing talent. Since 1953 readers have been treated to the thoughts of all-star instructors Bob Toski, the late Davis Love Jr., Jim Flick, Peter Kostis, Hank Haney, David Leadbetter, DeDe Owens, Chuck Cook, Bob Rotella and Harvey Penick, to name but a few. On the playing side, Byron Nelson, Sam Snead, Jack Nicklaus, Tom Watson, Lee Trevino, Tom Kite, Seve Ballesteros, Nick Faldo, Nick Price, Amy Alcott, Nancy Lopez and Patty Sheehan have all at one time or another laid bare their swing thoughts for the benefit of Golf Digest subscribers. And we're only scratching the surface; the complete list of contributors is as long as your straight left arm.

So you see where this book is coming from. Golf Digest is

the bible of golf instruction, the most respected name in the game when it comes to improving your scores. We at the magazine are justifiably proud of that reputation. We're proud to have done our bit to improve the quality of fairway life for more than a few over the last four decades. But—there's always a but—the fact remains: golfers still slice. A lot of golfers. One Golf Digest Schools Instructor estimates that as many as 85% of all players hit the ball from left-to-right with every club in the bag longer than a 9-iron (no figures are available on those who slice with the wedge!).

That's a sad state of affairs and one that needs to be rectified sooner rather than later. Slicing is golf's cancer and needs to be stopped. If you are one of the many sufferers, it no doubt goes without saying that you're tired of hitting those weak, left-to-right pop-ups into the right rough and trees. You're tired of being picked on by vindictive architects whose design theories always include lots of trouble down the right hand side of the fairway.

All of which is why you're reading this book.

Here's another, more positive reason. For the first time ever, the combined talents of those famous names mentioned earlier—and many others—have been brought together in one volume to cure your slice. That's what makes this book unique. It is the most illustrious group ever assembled to kill off slicing. If they can't cure it no one can.

So, if the thought of standing up on the 18th tee confident in the knowledge that the last thing you are about to do is slice sounds appealing, read on. Salvation is at hand.

For my Dad,
who drove all those miles when I was young and keen.

"I am the captive of my slice
I am the servant of my score"

SPORTSWRITER GRANTLAND RICE

1. Why people slice

At the beginning is always a good place to start an analysis of anything. If you hand a golf club to someone who has never hit a ball before and show him how to hold the club, he'll—nine times out of ten—set up to the shot amazingly well. At least in terms of alignment. He won't aim miles left or miles right; most of the time he will naturally stand pretty square to his target. Why? Because he doesn't have any past history to go on. He hasn't hit any bad shots yet, either right or left. So without thinking he just aims where he wants the ball to go.

Ten shots later things might be very different. If he's like most people he's worried about getting the ball into the air. He doesn't want to embarrass himself by scuttling the ball along the ground. Plus, he doesn't yet trust the loft on the club. So he tries to "scoop" the ball up.

In following that scenario, our new golfer has skipped a lesson. Getting the ball off the ground has to come after learning how to cock and uncock his wrists properly. And that means he has to learn that the loft on the club can only do its job correctly after the club lands a *descending* blow on the ball. Right now, of course, that's the last thing he's going to do. So he tries to help the ball up.

Pretty soon, he's hitting the ball way right of where he wants it to go. His scooping action is leaving the clubface wide open at impact and he's slicing every shot. It doesn't take him long to get tired of that, of course, and so he starts to aim left to allow for the left-to-right shots he's hitting. Then he discovers that he can further "help" the shot up by using his upper body to get the club "under" the ball. It isn't long before he's coming over the top (of which much more later) of every shot. And not long after that he's a fully paid up member of the slicers club.

Where did he go wrong? Well, he should have invested in a few lessons where he would have learned that the first step in golf is not how to get the ball airborne, it's how to get the ball airborne *properly*.

The previous scenario can also be encapsulated by the following: **most golfers slice because they are overly concerned with hitting the golf ball, not swinging the golf club.** And swinging the club properly comes from using all parts of your anatomy correctly. Sure, you can hit little shots straight just by using your hands and arms, but in a full-blooded drive your body has to play a part, too. If you can't use your body correctly,

When the club travels across the intended target line from out-to-in, the face open, sidespin is created which bends the ball to the right as its forward impetus decreases.

THE SLICE

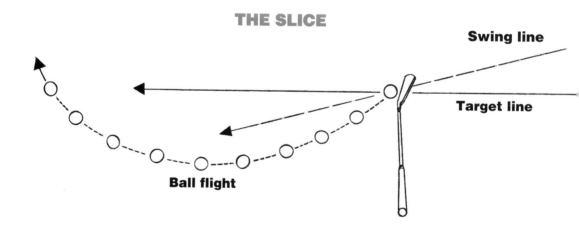

Swing line

Target line

Ball flight

your hands and arms are never going to be allowed to work properly either.

Think of it this way. If you are spinning a stone round and round on the end of a piece of string, the stone will stay in the same orbit as long as your forearm stays steady. If your forearm slows down, the stone moves out of its orbit and begins to work outward, away from the center. The same is true in your golf swing. If the shaft or clubhead is moving out from your body it's also moving across, so you're going to slice the shot. Thus, it's true that most people, by misinterpreting the role of the body in the golf swing, overuse it. Which means they don't use the club enough.

A straight shot: this time the club-head swings into the ball from inside the target line, moves along it, then back inside. It never gets "outside the line."

So take a look around you next time you're on the range, especially at those who habitually slice. It's a fact that none of them use their bodies even close to correctly. The opposite is also true. Take a peek at any good players in the line. Why don't they slice? Because they all use their bodies correctly.

That not everyone slices for the same reason is probably the last thing you wanted to hear. Sure, the end result is the same— that infuriatingly weak floater into the right rough—it's just that

THE STRAIGHT SHOT

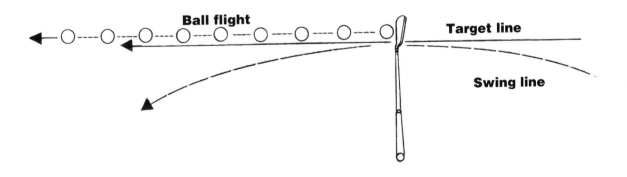

Ball flight

Target line

Swing line

the processes are different.

The real downside, of course, is that there is no one magical cure; no one single solution that will eliminate the banana ball forever; no one swing thought or drill that will rid all slicers of the problem. In fact, the causes and cures vary dramatically from one golfer to the next, making many "foolproof" slice cures obsolete.

The root cause of a slice is an open clubface in relation to your swing path through impact. The solution is a square or slightly closed clubface as it contacts the ball. However, your physical build or your perception of how your swing should look or feel can be the reason your clubface is habitually staying open. Any correction can only be made by taking these highly individualistic factors into account.

Having said that, according to Peter Kostis, slicers can be broken down into four main types:

1. *The Pull-Down Twister,* the golfer who perceives wrongly that golf is an entirely left-sided game.
2. *The One-Way Turner,* a wide-bodied person who doesn't turn sufficiently.
3. *The One-Piece Uplifter,* the frail, weak golfer who lacks the strength necessary to square the clubface.
4. *The Up-and-Down Bobber,* the player with an exceptionally tall or short spine who sets up to the ball incorrectly.

Let's look at each in turn:

1. *The Pull-Down Twister (p. 18).* The notion that the left-side "controls" the swing has produced countless slicers. It's easy to recognize this person at address: He positions the ball too far forward, with the left hand set even with or ahead of the ball; his right hand rides well on top of the left; his left arm is overly tight and rigid.

At the start of the swing, this golfer pushes the club straight back along the line of play, resulting in an arms-only, no-turn backswing. On the forward swing he pays for the errors he made at address, because his high right-hand position puts his right shoulder too high as well. As he pulls down with the left shoulder on the downswing, the right shoulder spins out and over the ball. Result: an outside-to-in swingpath with the clubhead trailing behind his hands. At impact the clubface is open and the ball must slice.

2. *The One-Way Turner (p. 20).* Some people are unable to pivot fully because of bulky builds. If you are overweight, have a big chest, a short neck, short arms or are simply not very supple, it's difficult for you to make a full shoulder turn and an uninhibited arm swing.

Chances are you compensate by merely using your arms. Without your body doing its part, the club gets badly out of position just before you start down. One of two errors result: You'll either try to square the clubface on the downswing by turning your body too much, leaving the clubhead far behind the handle and the clubface open at impact; or, you'll make a feeble attempt to route the club on the correct path with your arms, resulting in an outside-to-inside swing. Either way, a tremendous slice will result.

3. *The One-Piece Uplifter (p. 21).* Women constitute the largest percentage of this type of slicer, but many men fall into the category, too. They set up to the ball too upright because they can't stand the stress that proper posture exerts on their thighs and stomach. Furthermore, standard-weight clubs are too heavy for them and they swing very upright because the club feels lighter that way. Their swing has very little body rotation and their arms

Here's your typical slicer. Ball too far forward at address, left arm stiff, causing him to swing the club back too straight, before he comes "over the top" on the downswing.

become disconnected from the body as they swing along an outside-to-in path. Their lack of strength also prevents them from squaring the clubface, further guaranteeing a weak slice.

4. *The Up-and-down Bobber (p. 22)*. By setting your spine too upright or bending too far over the ball, you'll instinctively make mid-swing adjustments that lead to a slice. Poor posture is common among exceptionally tall or short golfers who think they must set up to the ball differently due to their height.

Actually, everyone's spine angle should be fairly similar. For a driver, that angle is about 27 degrees from upright, looking down the line from behind the golfer. Your spine angle becomes more upright as you progress through the other clubs.

The spine angle should remain constant throughout the swing. Raising or pitching forward can cause an outside-to-in swingpath and an open clubface. Here's why:

The short-spined golfer tends to set his spine too upright at address, lowering himself to the ball by flexing his knees and widening his stance. As a result of this posture, his weight shifts to his heels during the backswing, and he corrects by pitching forward on the downswing. This results in the classic "over the top" motion with the clubhead straying outside the target line and cutting across the ball through impact. He slices every time.

A tall, long-spined person is prone to bend over too far to reach the ball. His hands are too low, his legs too straight, his stance too narrow. As a result, his weight is positioned too far forward on his toes. To keep his balance on the backswing, he raises his spine. With his spine too upright as he begins the downswing, he pulls the butt end of the club through the hitting area first, leaving the clubhead trailing behind. At impact the clubface is open.

The "one-way turner," because of his build, can't make a full shoulder turn or use his arms properly.

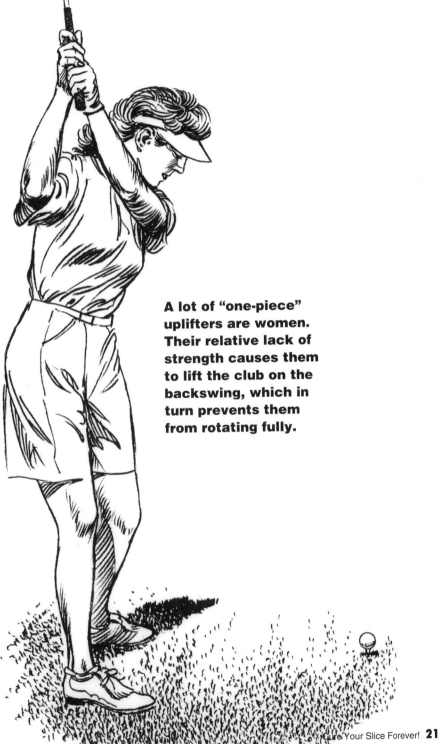

A lot of "one-piece" uplifters are women. Their relative lack of strength causes them to lift the club on the backswing, which in turn prevents them from rotating fully.

The "up-and-down bobber" slices because his poor posture at address causes him to either lift or dip during the swing. Both leave the clubface open at impact.

Whatever category or categories you fall into, there are some common factors in all of the above. It should be clear to you that **every slice stems originally from a fault or faults at address.** Those faults then translate into swing problems. The most common is an inability to swing the club into the ball on either the correct inside path or the correct angle. In other words, the club is traveling across the ball from out-to-in at impact and is also arriving on too steep an angle. Both are guaranteed to cause a slice.

The following chapters will fix all of those faults, not by focusing on the negatives in your present swing, but by presenting you with clear explanations of how to make a swing that will produce a straight shot or, alternatively, one that bends from right-to-left. Working on the drills outlined in each chapter will further enhance your feel for what is *right*, thus killing off the wrong.

How far you have to go with these drills—and how many you have to use—will be dictated by the severity of your slice. The cures or medicines on offer get stronger with each chapter.

Get to it.

"Setting up is ninety percent of good shotmaking."
JACK NICKLAUS, GOLF MY WAY.

2. Pre-swing

Most slicers are condemned to hit the shot to the right before the club ever moves away from the ball. Whether it is your grip, stance, aim, posture, or a combination of the above which is the root cause, you have ignored the first basic rule of golf: What you introduce at address is usually what you get at impact.

Now, if you've played golf for any amount of time—and if you're slicing so badly that you opened this book, you have— you've heard that line before. Probably over and over. Yet, paradoxically, it continues to be true that most bad shots are caused by faulty address positions. Players, for whatever reason, just don't listen to advice on the setup. Maybe it's because the fundamentals of anything tend to be boring. Maybe it's impatience; people just don't want to get worse before they get better.

It's like being told that servicing your car regularly will, in the long term, save you time and money. You know it's true, but you continue to skip getting it done because it's inconvenient. Then, when you break down on the highway in the middle of nowhere at two in the morning, you're kicking yourself for not doing something about it sooner. For the slicer, every tee shot is that empty highway at 2 a.m.

It's the same with the setup. Every golfer has been told how important it is, accepts the validity of the message, yet continues to neglect it. So, like the car, it continues to break down at the most inopportune moments. How many times have you stood on

This is how most slices start. The player sets up to the ball with his right side "high" at address. His body is aligned well left of the target.

the last tee needing to get the ball in the fairway, then sliced into trouble? Too many to count? Then it's time for a service.

The ultimate irony, of course, is that **the setup, being basically static, is something anyone can do perfectly.** Anyone. There is absolutely no good reason why even the humblest 28-handicapper, who on a good day can only just break 100, cannot position himself to hit the ball as well as the number one golfer in the world. All you have to be is a reasonable mimic.

And that is the aim of this chapter: to give you the sort of address position which will afford you the best possible chance of making a good golf swing. The sort of setup which will banish that slice forever.

Here's where we are right now. **Most slicers, as we've already seen in Chapter 1, set up to the ball with their right sides—shoulder and arm—higher than their left.** In other words, too far forward and too close to the ball-target line. Most grip the club too tightly. Most aim well to the left of their target. Most have the clubface closed (aligned left) to where they want the ball to finish. Each one of these typical characteristics is almost guaranteed to cause a slice. And when they're grouped together there is absolutely no question about where the ball is going: to the right.

So, although you've no doubt heard this many times before, the first thing you need if you want to get rid of that infernal banana ball is a fundamentally sound address position. Without that, you're always going to be fighting yourself. You cannot consistently start the ball at your target without a proper setup. And it's not that hard to learn if you are patient and methodical in your approach. Pre-swing positions are easy to observe and check because they are just that: positions. The lack of movement actually works to your advantage.

Let's look at each aspect in turn.

Grip

Most instruction books start off with a detailed description of the three most common ways in which you can attach your hands to the club: the overlapping, interlocking or ten-finger grips. Not this one. Whatever grip you want to use is fine. All three can work equally well. Just use the one you find most comfortable. It's entirely up to you.

What is important is the position of your hands relative to one another. Your palms must always be parallel. Take a look at your grip in a mirror. What does it look like? Is your right hand high on top of the grip, the 'V' between thumb and forefinger

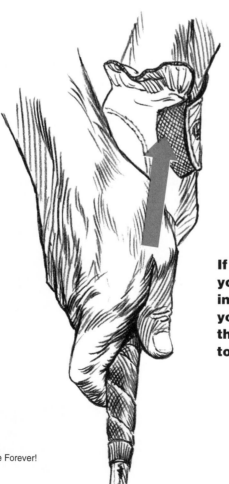

If the 'v' formed by your right thumb and index finger points to your left shoulder, then your right hand is too high on the club.

pointing at your left shoulder? If so, you have just identified one cause of your inability to rotate your arms in the swing: a weak grip *(p. 28)*. So called because it prevents your hands, arms and body from moving quickly. And if they're moving slowly, so is your clubhead.

Try this drill *(p. 30)* for proof. Let your arms hang in front of you and place your right palm over the back of your left hand and interlock the fingers. When you try to make a swing, you'll immediately notice how tense you are and how difficult it is to make any kind of proper arm rotation. That's how your weak grip chokes your swing; no wonder it contributes to a slice.

Such a weak grip causes other problems, too. When your right hand is high on the club, your right arm is higher than your left arm, your right shoulder is higher than your left shoulder and your upper body is automatically open in relation to the target line. All of which, of course, is hardly designed to foster either an on-plane swing or a right-to-left ball flight.

Instead, you need a grip that is going to encourage your right side to be lower than your left side at address; that is going to make it easier for your right side to turn out of the way on the backswing; and that is going to make it easier for you to rotate the clubface from open to square to closed on the downswing and follow through. The grip that best fills those particular roles is one in which **both hands are turned clockwise on the club until the 'V's' between both thumbs and forefingers point at your right shoulder and the fleshy pad at the base of your left thumb is on top of the club** *(p. 31)*. When you look down you should see at least two and maybe three knuckles on the back of your left hand. Any more is too much; any less not enough.

Such a grip, in golfing terms, is "strong." Sure, it is still possible to slice the ball holding the club this way, but not if you combine it with the swinging and turning motion you'll learn in Chapter 3. The bottom line? Slicing the ball is just much harder to do if you have a strong grip. Certainly, you can block it or push it to the right by not allowing your hands to release through impact—"holding on" to the shot—but actually curving the ball from left-to-right in the air is more difficult.

Having said all that, what a strong grip can't be is tight. That, in terms of ridding yourself of a slice, is the most important

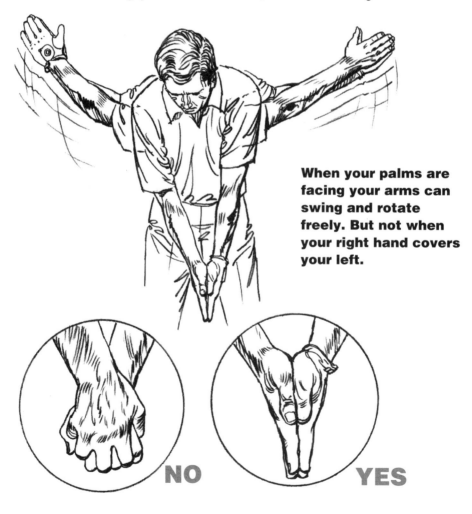

When your palms are facing your arms can swing and rotate freely. But not when your right hand covers your left.

NO

YES

aspect of your grip. Holding the club in a death grip can literally strangle the life out of your hands—and game.

In order to get the ball flying straight or right-to-left in the air your hands have to play their part. If they can't work properly an insidious chain reaction is set off. Up through your wrists and arms it creeps, up into your shoulders. The end result is a stiffness and tension in your whole upper body that inhibits any kind

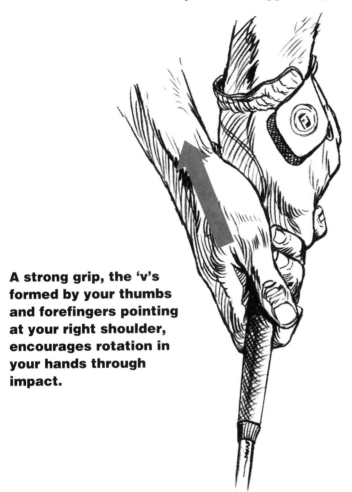

A strong grip, the 'v's formed by your thumbs and forefingers pointing at your right shoulder, encourages rotation in your hands through impact.

of turning or releasing of the club through impact. It is a physiological fact that **tight, constricted muscles do not operate as well as relaxed, elongated muscles.** Try running 50 yards with your legs stiff and tense and you'll know how much of your potential speed is wasted.

So you need a relaxed but firm hold on the club if you are to make a free and easy swing. Without the former, you'll never make the latter. It's that important. Greg Norman won the 1986 British Open at Turnberry in Scotland focusing solely on grip pressure, especially toward the end of his round when the inclination to hold on tight was greatest.

How to find your proper grip pressure

How light is light? Lighter than you think, probably. **It is virtually impossible to start the swing with a grip that is loose,** even if you think it is. So exaggerate things at first. If you think your grip is loose, it's probably just right. If you think it feels light, you're in all likelihood still holding on too tightly. And, even worse, if you think you're gripping firmly, the death hold is back.

But you need a reference point. These four Bob Toski exercises will help you identify how lightly you can hold the club while still maintaining control of it.

Take your grip while pointing the club straight up in front of your face. Keep your grip pressure as light as possible, just firm enough to support the club. Then gradually lower the club to a horizontal position, keeping your grip light and your muscles relaxed. Without conscious effort your grip will tighten only enough to support the club.

While walking, hold the club in your left hand and swing it to and fro around your body, keeping your muscles in a relaxed state and applying only enough pressure with the last three fingers to keep the handle snug against your palm. This demonstrates the freedom of motion you can achieve with a light, relaxed grip.

Holding the club in a horizontal position, have a partner grasp the clubhead end and push, pull and twist the club back and forth, slowly but with some force *(p. 34)*. You grasp the club only with enough firmness to keep it from turning or sliding in your hands. You'll be surprised how little force it takes from you to maintain control of the club.

Assume your top of the backswing position with your left hand only controlling the club. If you find this too difficult, help support the club with your right hand but exert no pressure with it. Loosen the last three fingers of your left hand, letting the clubhead droop slightly, then slowly re-grip. This will identify how little pressure you need to maintain control at the top.

Having identified a light grip, now try to hit a dozen or so shots while holding the club as lightly as possible. If you're doing it correctly, your slice should not be nearly as severe as before. Then hit a dozen while gripping the club as tightly as you can. In all probability your slice will be as bad as ever.

Next, return to your lightest possible grip as you address a shot, then firm it up slightly, only to the extent you need to control the club. If you feel uneasy about gripping so lightly, you can build a slight feeling of control into the last three fingers of your left hand. But remember this one important point—your grip pressure will tighten instinctively as you begin to take the club away and will continue to do as the speed of the swing increases.

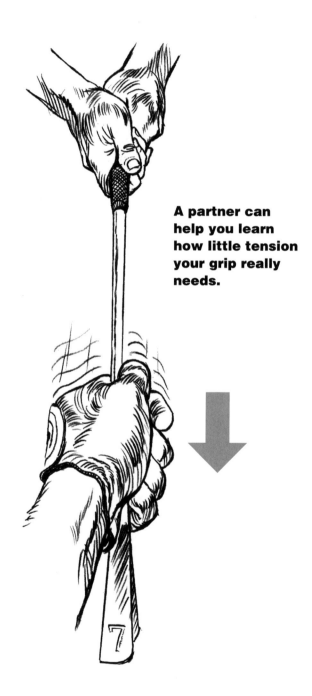

A partner can help you learn how little tension your grip really needs.

Aim/Alignment

OK, now that you are holding the club with the grip least likely to encourage a slice and your grip pressure has decreased to the point where your hands can work effectively, it's time to work on your aim and alignment. After all, you can hardly expect the ball to get to the target on a consistent basis if your body and club are pointing somewhere else.

Until now, the vital parts of your anatomy—shoulders, hips, feet—have all been aligned to the left of the target. That's a safe assumption because there aren't many slicers out there aiming to the right. Can you imagine where their shots would end up? In spots which quickly encourage them to aim left to allow for their left-to-right ball flight. The delights of the rough, bunkers and trees down the right hand side of every hole quickly pale for even the most stubborn.

Let's start from the ground up with the clubface. Set a 2-by-4 piece of wood on the ground outside your ball, parallel with and to the right of your ball-target line *(p. 36)*. Draw a perpendicular line across the middle of the board, at right angles to the target line. Use a pencil, marking back and forth, to highlight the middle groove on the face of your 5-iron. Now address a ball so that you match up the line on the board with the darkened groove. When you have done that, you know your clubface is aligned squarely to the target.

But wait a minute. Feels strange, right? Well, of course, it does. All the time you've been slicing the clubface has been aligned somewhere other than the target. So what was wrong looked square to you. And what is correct is going to look wrong—at least at first. It's going to take time to get used to such a new look. So take that time. Repeat this exercise over and over until the clubface looks correct to you sitting squarely behind the ball.

Once you can place the clubhead squarely behind the ball every time you're ready to match your body to the clubface. That means aligning your feet, knees, hips and shoulders on a line that is parallel with but left of the ball-target line. Again, let's start from the ground up.

Make things easy for yourself. Address your ball again. Now place a club along your toeline. Step back. Where is it pointing? Are it and the 2-by-4 parallel? Probably not. So make them parallel *(p. 37)*.

Address the ball again, this time with your toes hard against

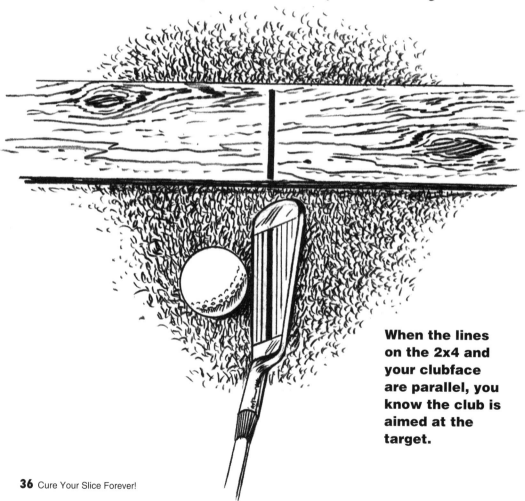

When the lines on the 2x4 and your clubface are parallel, you know the club is aimed at the target.

Practice placing your feet against the shaft on the ground. You won't feel square to the target, but you are.

the shaft on the ground. Again, it looks and feels weird, right? Your feet are the same as your clubface. Because you've been misaligned for so long you've forgotten what square looks like. Don't fall into that trap again. Stand to the ball as many times as it takes you to get used to this new feel. And be patient with yourself. Lining up to the target is never easy.

When you have your feet square to the target, it's a fair bet that your knees are the same way. You'd have to be a contortionist to get your lower body too far out of line when your feet are square.

The same, however, cannot be said of the upper body. A great many players already have a square clubface at address and align their lower bodies parallel to that face. But still they slice. Why? Because their upper bodies are aligned to the left, the right shoulder far too close to the ball-target line *(p. 39)*.

The reason why this problem continues to plague so many slicers is too much focusing on the effect—coming over the top of the ball with the shoulders early in the downswing, imparting an out-to-in glancing blow on the ball and then watching it bend from left-to-right—rather than the cause—poor upper body alignment.

Use your spine as your reference point here. Get someone to stand behind you at address. Ideally, your spine should be very close to vertical. Only the fact that your right hand is lower on the club than your left should cause it to tilt ever so slightly to your right. **If you can maintain the angle of your spine throughout your swing the clubhead will have a greater chance of returning to the ball squarely along the correct inside-to-square-to-inside swing path.**

Should your spine stray from this near perpendicular position, your swing path and ball flight will change dramatically. Why? The spine is an axis around which the shoulders turn and

Ideally, your spine should tilt only very slightly to the right at address.

If your spine tilts to the left at address, you are well on the way to slicing the shot.

the arms swing freely. Since your swing path tends to be from out-to-in it is clear that your spine has most likely been listing to the left. Get it back to near vertical and you know that your upper body is back in line with your lower half. And, more importantly, you know that you are finally lined up squarely with your target.

You can't make a
balanced swing if your
weight is too far forward
on your toes (or too far
back on your heels)
at address.

If your weight is
centered on the
balls of your feet,
you'll be able to
rock from heel
to toe without
falling over.

Posture

The body angles you create at address are a major influence on both the shape of your swing and the shape of your shots. There are a few basics you should be aware of. David Leadbetter contends that you want your weight "underneath" you, on the balls of your feet, not forward on your toes as it would be if your legs are too straight; or back on your heels as it would be if your legs were too bent.

Most slicers, however, tend to place too much weight on their toes. Why? Two main reasons: (1) the fact that you naturally have to bend forward at address, and (2) the attraction of the ball—players tend to be "drawn" toward it.

Check yourself in a mirror. If you look anything like the larger character depicted on the opposite page, then your weight isn't where it should be. You'll have little chance of making a fluid, balanced swing and so will be forced into unnecessary compensations later.

Instead, try to feel light on your feet. Flex your knees—but only slightly. Bend forward from your hips. Then let your arms hang freely from your shoulders. That is an athletic and tension-free setup.

Test yourself. **If you are well-balanced, your weight on the balls of your feet, you should be able to rock back and forward from heel to toe without tipping over.**

You want to maintain that posture as you turn your body back and through in the swing. If you are set properly at address, there is no need to contort yourself once the swing begins. After all, you might as well get things right at the start.

Ball position

Here's another test, devised by Hank Haney. Set three balls on the ground as shown *(p. 43)*. Pick up your 5-iron and ask yourself which one you presently find easiest to hit. If you like B, fine. But if you are a typical slicer you're going to find ball C a bit more attractive.

If ball C is your preferred position, the ball and bottom of your swing are too far forward. Whether they got there to fit your swing shape or your swing shape altered to fit your ball position is, at this stage, immaterial. Confine yourself to the two possible causes of your slice. You could be swinging the club down on a steep, outside-the-line path—coming over the top— or your hands are simply failing to release through impact.

When the ball is too far forward, your upper body is pulled out toward the target line, aligning both the shoulders and club-face well left of where you want the ball to go (sound familiar?). So you need to get from C to B. And stay there. It isn't enough simply to move the ball back. Habits are hard to break. It's only a matter of time before you creep forward again.

Here's how to get more comfortable with the correct ball position. Address a ball in position B. Then square up your left foot and flare out your right *(p. 44)*. This makes it easier for you to turn on the backswing, then inhibit your body turn on the downswing (it isn't a bad idea to incorporate this flaring out of your right foot into your regular address position). Try to release your hands and the clubhead more from the top of the swing, as if the ball is in position A. In other words, exaggerate the feeling. You'll soon be hitting the ball from right to left and be a lot more comfortable with the ball in position B.

Pre-shot routine

So far we've made a lot of changes and you haven't even hit a ball in anger yet. You're going to have to be patient with yourself. Almost every aspect of your setup is now different and it'll take time to get used to all those new looks and feels. You need

Pullers and slicers of the ball tend to prefer ball position 'C,' which is too far forward.

To make ball position 'B' more comfortable, square up your left foot and flare out your right.

Imagining you are hitting the ball in position 'A,' turn your body on the backswing, then release your hands and arms on the through-swing.

TURN

A   B   C

some discipline, too. Make yourself address a ball, say, 20 times every day until the new feelings are ingrained. Start from the beginning every time; don't get sloppy. Remember, good shots start with a good setup. Which is why you're going to need a sound, ordered preshot routine.

Every top player has a preshot routine. Actually, preshot discipline would be a better phrase. **They don't hit the ball until they are happy that all aspects of their address position are as they should be.** Neither, of course, should you.

This book isn't going to give you a specific physical routine to work through, though. You need to devise your own. Just don't make it too involved or long. You'll either forget something or annoy the hell out of your playing companions or, more likely, the group behind!

According to Dr. Bob Rotella, what you do need, however, is a mental preshot routine. Many players think a preshot routine is all physical. Wrong. You can physically go through the steps of a routine, but if your mind is wandering it won't be any good—especially when you're under pressure.

Your preshot routine is that important. Some people think that impact is the "moment of truth." Maybe. The point where it's time to move your body is the real moment of truth. You better believe in yourself when you take the club back—and stay in that mode through impact.

Golf is such an honest game it's going to expose your every doubt. If you always blame slices on your swing you never answer the real question: Was your mind in the right place? It's OK to hit less than perfect shots, but good players make sure they are not caused by doubt. They eliminate slices due to bad thoughts. Then they accept their shortcomings and move on.

So be honest. Know whether your mind is in a good place or a bad place when you pull the trigger. Don't kid yourself. A lot of people walk around very proud of themselves. They think they have a great preshot routine. But too often they don't. They've got all the moves: the practice swing, the waggles, the looks at the target. But those aren't enough if your mind is still on how you "sliced on this hole yesterday."

Every aspect of your routine has to suit your temperament and physique. Then you have to do it enough that it becomes effortless and automatic and puts your mind in the right place. Which takes patience. It must become a habit. And that takes repetition—both mental and physical. It's no good trying something four or five times, then when it doesn't work right away, saying, "I tried those routines and they're useless."

Build a dominant habit

Some players, to get themselves aligned squarely with the target, simply pull the club from the bag while standing beside the ball. Others stand behind the ball looking at the hole. And there are those who don't look at the target until they're set up. All are OK. As long as you are doing what is right for you. The key is that you be comfortable with it, that it gets you aimed correctly and that you trust that aim.

Find out which category you are in. Walk in from behind the ball and have someone check your alignment. Do that 10 times and see how good your aim is. Then try it the other ways. Or, indeed, any way you like. As long as you do what is right for you.

Once you know your own tendencies, never deviate. Don't be influenced by others. Don't use an intermediate target because Jack Nicklaus did; use it because it helps you. And once you are comfortable with your aim, forget about it. Focus on the target.

Line up the same way enough times and it becomes a habit. Then a dominant habit. You want your dominant habit to hold up on holes where you used to slice into trouble every time. If your dominant habit is pointless, under pressure your mind will wander.

Monitor your routine in practice to be sure that you are not getting sloppy. Catch problems early before they start affecting your play in competition. Then keep doing what you're doing.

Analyze the best part of your game

Ask yourself what the strongest part of your game is. Then get someone to watch or film you preparing to hit those shots. Next, identify the weakest part of your game (be honest!). Then get your friend to repeat his analysis.

Are there any differences in your preshot routine? If you're like most people there will be. If you're like most people your strength will have an identifiable preshot pattern to it. You'll make the same number of waggles, looks at the target or whatever. And you'll take the same amount of time over each shot. In other words, you'll go through the same "unthinking" mental and physical routine each time.

Contrast that with the shot you really don't fancy too much, say, the drive on that hole with the lake on the right hand side. The number of waggles changes. You peek at the hole more often. You take a lot longer to get "ready." You're like a different person.

The solution? Discipline yourself. Make yourself incorporate your "good" preshot routine into your weakest shots.

"On the backswing, the order of movement goes like this: hands, arms, shoulders, hips. On the downswing the order is reversed: hips, shoulders, arms, hands."

BEN HOGAN, THE MODERN FUNDAMENTALS OF GOLF.

3. How to turn—both back and through

Your turn is the place where most of your slices are born, and yet it's in the turn where we'll cure most slices. In this chapter we'll explore how your shoulders turn correctly, how the rest of your body turns to complement your shoulders, and how the right drills and images can help you put those elements together in the correct sequence.

THE SHOULDERS AND THE TURN

Your shoulders do most of the turning in your golf swing and, as should be clear from the previous chapter, they can either be your enemies or your friends. The biggest problem in striking a golf ball to your target is an inability to swing the club on the correct path. **Overactive shoulders force the club off that correct path and cause your slices,** especially when those shoulders start out of position at address.

You've already seen what placing the right shoulder too close to the target line does to your alignment at address, but its effect on both your backswing and downswing is even more disastrous.

Focus more on making a good turn than on fixing your previous fault. Trying to *do* something is easier than trying *not to do* something else. So be positive. Look at it this way: If you can make a proper turn, then you won't have to worry about making an improper one. So whether you are the type of slicer who picks the club outside the line (above the plane) on the backswing then drops it down the same way, or more of the whip it inside (below the plane) then over the top (above the plane) kind of guy, the "fix" is the same: a swingpath that is on-plane.

A right shoulder that is too high at address makes it all but impossible for you to turn properly on the backswing. You simply can't get out of your own way.

When you get it right, your shoulder turn should feel a bit like a coiling of your upper body *over* your lower body. In other words, as your lower body provides resistance, your shoulders turn to the point where the left shoulder is under your chin. It is that combination of resistance and coiling that creates the potential for clubhead speed through impact.

The shoulders also have a great influence on the path of the club. **If you can't turn, you can't get the club around you on the backswing.** All you can do is lift it up in the air. Put no turn and an outside-the-line backswing together and you're well on the way to a slice. Conversely, it pays not to overreact by turning excessively. Overturning gets the club too much to the inside early in the backswing, leaving you with only one way to go on the downswing: over the top.

However, having said that, by squaring up your address position you're already halfway to avoiding either of those dire scenarios. Now you have to learn how to turn properly. To do that you have to go on the offense. It, after all, is the best form of defense.

A golf shot is the result of the shape of your swing and how it matches your setup. Now, having made a fairly major alteration to your address position already, you have to make the swing to match. If you can create the right swing shape to go with the right setup, then you're going to hit a successful shot. Let's look first at the way your body must turn or pivot during the swing. It is the foundation of your swing, around which everything else must move. Thus, **it is your pivot that largely determines the shape of your swing.** It is your pivot that allows your hands and arms to work properly.

ELEMENTS OF A PROPER TURN

1. Balance is key

The proper swing begins with proper balance. At address the insides of your heels should be about shoulder-width apart. Then, as we said in Chapter 2, you need to have your weight distributed so that if somebody were to stand in front of you and push both shoulders back toward your heels, you wouldn't lose your balance backward. And if somebody stood behind you and pushed, you wouldn't fall forward either. From a face-on view there should basically be a 50-50 distribution of weight on each foot, with a slight bit more, perhaps, on the right leg, because of the tilting of the spine ever so slightly to the right.

2. A correct pivot

The correct pivot is one that revolves around the spine, with the shoulders feeling as if they're turning perpendicular to the spine angle. Peter Kostis says that the best way to learn this is to practice turning with a bar across your shoulders *(p. 52)*. A ball

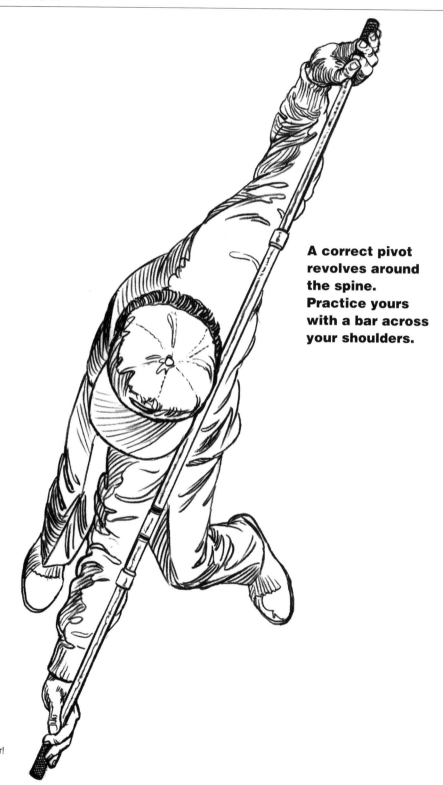

A correct pivot revolves around the spine. Practice yours with a bar across your shoulders.

retriever or broomstick will work, too. The aim is to maintain a constant shoulder plane in your pivot, both away from and back to the ball.

Don't worry if, when you first practice this move, it feels as if you are reverse pivoting (your weight moving to your left side on the backswing, to the right side on the downswing). As long as you set up with your spine slightly to the right of the golf ball and turn around your spine, then you'll be sufficiently "behind the ball." This proper shoulder turn will help with the rest of your body turning, too.

3. Start back all at once

A word about bringing the correct pivot to a real golf swing: Once you get a club in your hands and repeat the turn you're practicing, it's important to understand that the pivot should be starting at the same instant the clubhead starts back from the ball (p. 55). Actually, although everything starts at the same time, the parts are moving at different speeds, which gives the appearance of starting one part ahead of another. Here's an illustration: If you line up a Porsche, a Rolls Royce and a Mack truck, start the engines and give them a green light, they will start at the same time, but after a couple of feet, because they are going at different speeds, it will appear that the Porsche has started ahead of the Rolls, which will appear to have started ahead of the truck. That's why in the golf swing it looks like the clubhead and hands, which are lighter and faster, have started ahead of the hips and shoulders. Besides, they have to go faster because they have farther to travel.

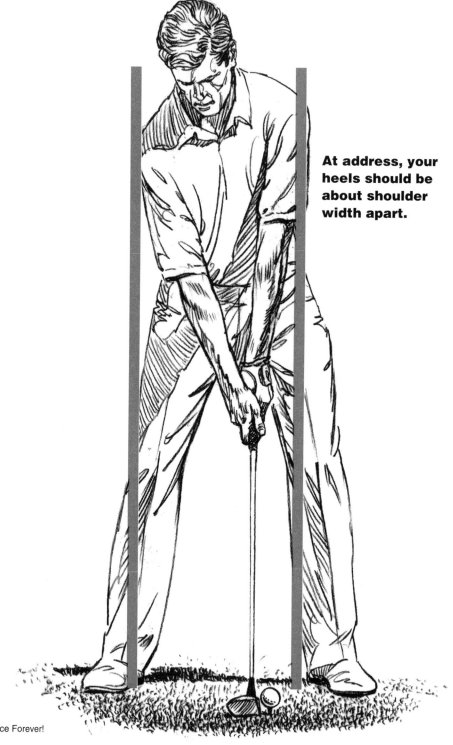

**At address, your
heels should be
about shoulder
width apart.**

Everything in your swing, hands, arms, shoulders, torso and club, should start back together.

4. Getting the right sequence in the turn

OK, you've now got some idea of the elements of a proper turn. But you've only felt them with a bar across your shoulders, not a club in your hands. Plus, there's no telling how strange a proper pivot is going to feel to you. It even feels different to good players. Ask 100 pros to describe their turns to you and you'll most likely get 100 different answers.

All of which makes the following drills even more important. Experiment with all of them, but discard the ones you're not comfortable with. There are no absolute rights and wrongs here; you have to feel your own way to an extent.

Having said that, it's time to get specific.

You're over the ball at address. Your setup is perfect; everything square to your target. Now what? Your inclination is still going to be to, say, lift the club outside the line as you did before, even if you have been practicing your bar drill. Most of the time you'll get it right, but occasionally that old lifting move, which you ingrained for years, is going to creep in. You need some reinforcement in the form of some checkpoints. You need to get your upper and lower halves working together.

The exercises and drills which follow in a moment will show you exactly where you and the club should be at the most vital stages of your swing. You'll also get to know how each part of your swing should *feel*. **Practice each of these drills one at a time. Don't move to the next one until you have mastered each.** Once you have a good feel for them all, or at least the ones you like, you'll be ready to put the whole thing together. Remember, your swing is not a succession of positions to be ticked off one after the other; it is a *swing through* those positions.

Over the top

This is one of the most common phrases in golf. And for good reason. It is the number one cause of slices. From the top of the swing, slicers tend to throw the club out from their bodies so that it approaches the ball from outside the target line *(see illustration below)*. That forces them to hit at the ball with their upper bodies, their right shoulders high through impact (there's that shoulder again). The result is a slice if the clubface is open at impact—it usually is—or a straight pull to the left if the face happens to be square. Either way, the result is not pretty.

The number one cause of slicing is coming "over the top," the club thrown out, ---away from the body on the downswing.

The biggest problem, however, is your particular affliction. The club comes down so far from the outside that the weak slicing action across the ball prevents solid contact. A weak shot to the right—we can only say slice so many times—is the result.

But fear not, there is a cure for this. You just have to learn how to release the club earlier in the downswing. The key is your right arm, specifically the elbow. See how bent it is when you come over the top? There is no way to create any real power when you are so cramped and restricted. You have to hit *at* the ball rather than sweeping it away.

Contrast that with the correct position. **The right elbow has almost straightened and is close to the player's side, allowing him to swing through the ball from inside the ball-target line.**

Sense that your right arm is straightening from the very top of your swing. Then you can replace the excessive body motion you previously employed with a fast moving clubhead.

Practice prevents strain

Go back to practicing with the bar across your shoulders *(pp. 60-61)*. Practice the turn slowly at least 50 times a day until your muscles are stretched and you're able to make a full turn without any strain. If you don't lengthen your turn through exercise, you'll have so much tension in your swing that you'll lose rhythm and tempo.

Ideally, you should have a friend watch you swinging with the bar to make certain that it and your shoulders are turning perpendicular to the forward tilt of your spine. It's possible to do the drill in front of a mirror, but by looking up at your reflection you change your head position, which alters the spine angle slightly and keeps you from creating the correct tension and coil.

Remember that the angle of the swing plane changes with the shorter clubs. This is mainly the result of your posture changes. With the wedge, for example, your spine is more over the ball so your shoulder turn is more vertical and it's harder to make a full turn. As the clubs get longer, the pivot becomes greater and even more important. Which is one reason why you slice the driver more than, say, the 8-iron.

DRILLS FOR A PROPER BACKSWING

Shift left hip on takeaway

Thinking only in terms of turning the upper body behind the ball, without due concern for the lower body, can create a situation where the left hip does not turn or move away from its starting point.

Try this drill *(p. 62)*. Address a ball normally, a shaft stuck in the ground just outside your left heel so that the grip end rests against your left hip. As it turns away from the ball, your left hip should make a slight lateral move away from the shaft.

Use tee as checkpoint

It should be clear to you by now that the first move into the backswing is a combination of hands, arms, club and body moving together to the point where the shaft is horizontal. At that stage the back of your left hand and the clubface should be looking straight in front of you. When that is the case you know you are on-plane.

Make this your first checkpoint in the swing. Stick a tee in the hole in the back of your glove. If you pick the club up too steeply the tee will point down. If you fan the clubface open by taking the club away too much on the inside, the tee will point skyward. In both cases there is no togetherness between club,

Get someone to watch you turning. Your shoulders should turn perpendicular to the forward tilt of your spine on the backswing.

...and on the throughswing.

Stick a club shaft in the ground outside your left heel with the handle resting on your hip. As the club moves back from the ball, your hip should make a slight lateral shift away from the club.

hands and body. They are working independently.

Work on this little exercise until you can move the club away from the ball and get the tee pointing straight ahead *(p. 64)*. The toe of the club should be perpendicular when the shaft is horizontal.

To achieve that, your left arm must rotate slightly as your body, hands, arms and the club move away together. Practice this drill as often as you can. It encourages the proper blend of hand and body action early in the swing.

If you are still in good shape when the clubshaft is horizontal on the backswing, your chances of getting to the top without moving off-plane are significantly enhanced. But there is one more check you can make before you get to that stage.

When your left arm reaches horizontal the club should, if properly balanced, feel very light.

Try it and see. If you have to make a conscious effort to hold the club up, you're off-plane. Either the club is too far behind you or too far in front of you. So get into the position where the club feels lightest to you. Once there you just have to keep going to get into the "slot" at the top.

Check your turn in mirror

That's how the club should feel, but David Leadbetter's "mirror drill"*(p. 65)* is designed to give you a feel for the proper sequence of body moves in the backswing.

Without a club, adopt your normal address. Leaving your left arm in its original position, place your right hand on your left hip. Turn away from the ball by pulling your left hip back and across. Pull on it as your left arm and shoulder start to move. That introduces the slight lateral shift, which in turn allows your weight to move to your right side.

As this is happening, your left knee should move across to a

Use a tee stuck in the back of your glove as a checkpoint. In the correct takeaway, the tee should point straight ahead when the clubshaft is horizontal.

Pull your left hip back and across with your right hand while watching your turn in a mirror. This shows you the proper sequence of body moves on the backswing.

point where it looks at, or a little behind, the ball. Retain the flex in your right knee so there is no danger of you swaying off the ball.

Check that you have made a good backswing by turning and looking in the mirror. See how level your hips are. See how much of a turning, coiling motion you've made with your trunk. Feel how your weight is now concentrated primarily on your right heel.

Repeat this drill a few times and you will be well on the way to instinctively feeling the role that your upper and lower spine play in a good backswing.

Left heel up, right foot back

Once the mirror drill has given you a better idea of how your weight shift onto the right side should feel on the backswing, this drill will further ingrain that sensation. Place a club on the ground parallel to your target line. Address the ball normally, then pull your right foot back until your right toe is level with your left instep. Lift your left heel off the ground a fraction. Leave it there throughout the backswing. That will make it virtually impossible for you to exert any downward pressure on your left foot. These adjustments all encourage correct lower-spine movements—and shift your weight onto your right side.

When you move the club away from the ball, make a conscious effort to shift your weight to your right heel. There is only one proviso: Take care not to let your left knee move inward too much *(p. 67)*. Key on turning your trunk. That will get you moving into your right side sufficiently.

With your left heel off the ground, you want to maintain resistance in both knees, the right in particular, to prevent any loss of coil.

Again, repeat this drill until you are making the proper

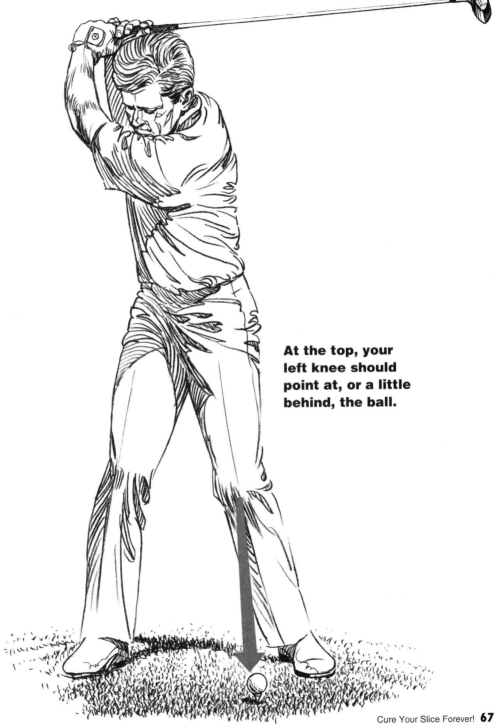

At the top, your left knee should point at, or a little behind, the ball.

moves instinctively.

Left shoulder 'replaces' right

A surefire way to ensure a full shoulder turn is to note in your mind's eye the position of your right shoulder at address. On the backswing, let your shoulders and hips respond to the swinging of your arms so that, at the top, your left shoulder occupies the space vacated by the right *(p. 69)*.

At the top

This three-step drill will further tell you how the top of your backswing should feel. From address, pick the club straight up and lay it on your left shoulder. Turn your hips and shoulders fully until you can see the ball out of the corner of your left eye. Extend your arms upward until your left arm is stretched. And there you have it: the perfect top of the backswing position.

DRILLS FOR A PROPER DOWNSWING

Start down uniformly

While it's true that the lower body starts forward fractionally ahead of the upper body at the beginning of the downswing, try to feel as if everything is starting down at the same time. But remember, the parts are traveling at different speeds, so you get the appearance of starting one part ahead of the other. Just try to feel as if you're getting a uniform start back and a uniform start down, without emphasizing any one part *(p. 70)*.

Drive a stake down from the top

This drill, devised by the late Davis Love Jr., will help you understand—and feel—the *down* in the downswing. It counteracts your slicer's tendency to start the downswing with the

At the top your left shoulder should fill the position your right shoulder did at address.

Don't emphasize any part of your anatomy at the start of the downswing. Just try to keep everything moving 'together.'

The key to the downswing is your right arm. Have the feeling that it's straightening, almost from the top of your swing. Halfway down your right elbow will then be close to your side.

Line up 3 balls on a 45-degree angle. If you can hit the middle ball without touching the others, your downswing is on the correct inside path.

shoulder twist to the left described in the previous drill.

You want your first move from the top of the backswing to be with your arms, wrists and hands swinging the club straight down. A good way to ingrain that feeling is by imagining you are going to drive a stake into the ground from the top of the backswing.

While this is more of a mental image than a drill, you might actually want to place a stake or clubshaft in the ground to help you achieve the downward feeling. Position it about a club-length off your right foot, at a height even with the middle of your body, along a line running through the arches of your feet and parallel to the target line.

To pound the stake into the ground, you would have to use your arms, wrist and hands (don't actually try it; you'll break your driver). Just return the club gently to the top of the stake to get the proper feel.

Hit the middle ball

Line up three balls on a 45-degree angle as shown in the illustration, opposite. The center ball is your target. Make sure there's enough space between each ball to swing the club through. Now make your swing and try to hit the middle ball. If you can do that without dislodging either of the other balls, you know that your club is approaching the ball from the correct inside path—not the outside as it was before you picked up this book.

Try to make your forearms touch

Typically, slicers don't release the clubhead through impact. They release it much too early in the downswing, losing the angle formed by the left arm and clubshaft almost from the top of the backswing. The longer you retain that angle, the more power you store prior to impact. In a good swing, release happens naturally, through centrifugal force. The clubhead gets heavier, in effect, as it's swung, and the wrists are unleashed at the right time.

To encourage all of that, try, as Tom Watson does, to release the club by rotating your forearms. **Try to touch your left forearm with your right forearm as you hit the ball.** When you're practicing, rotate your forearms as fast as you can in making this effort. Your forearms probably won't actually touch, but the thought will lead to a better release. Work on it and you'll stop leaving the clubface open at impact.

Now, even if you've worked diligently on all of these drills and exercises and have started to hit the ball close to straight, you've got a lot to think about. It'll be a while before you are making effortless passes at the ball. You may even be finishing off-balance just because your head is so full of swing mechanics. If it helps, summarize the swing as follows:

1) address–stay in balance
2) takeaway–back of left hand vertical when shaft is horizontal.
3) at the top–left shoulder "replaces" right
4) from the top–pound the stake into the ground
5) impact–hit the "middle" ball
6) follow through–make your forearms touch

Give yourself a break now and then. Shift your attention away from both the ball and the result of the shot. Instead, concentrate on swinging the club through the ball. Focus on your finish. Try to maintain as much acceleration as possible, all the way to the end of your follow through. Let the club's momentum carry it around your back. When you can hold this position for a few seconds, you'll know that your swing is balanced. Alternatively, go back to the bar drill you worked on originally. It will take your mind off positions and back onto making a complete *swing*. When you're doing that, you can start thinking about hitting the ball from right-to-left—the subject of the next chapter.

"If you slice, initially you have to exaggerate the factors that will produce a draw."

GARY PLAYER, GOLF BEGINS AT 50.

4. How to draw the ball

You should be approaching this chapter from one of two angles. Either you have mastered the turning motion described in the previous chapter and are now simply looking for a little more distance; or you're still having trouble turning and need some medicine that is a little stronger.

That increased dosage comes in the form of learning to draw the ball. Chapter 3 was designed to get you hitting the ball straight, here you're trying to move it from right-to-left in the air—the very antithesis of a slice.

The benefits of doing so are two-fold. Not only do you rid yourself of that slice, but you gain distance, too. Formal testing conducted separately by Golf Digest and the United States Golf Association indicates that a draw travels farther in all wind and turf conditions. A draw flies lower than a slice due to the clubface being slightly closed at impact, which causes the ball to descend on a less steep angle. This means more roll. Surprisingly, according to these tests, a draw also *flies* farther than a slice. The reason: although the ball flies lower, it is launched from the clubface with more forward momentum, so it stays in the air longer.

The muscle tension created in your left side by a slightly open stance helps you rotate your hips more quickly on the downswing.

Slightly open stance creates
a powerful downswing

There is a popular notion that the open stance you formerly employed can only produce a slice, not a draw. Maybe, says Scott Davenport of the Golf Digest Schools. Your shoulders and hips *must* be square at address, to produce a correct backswing. Your stance, however, is a different matter. If you open your stance by bringing your left foot away from the target line slightly at address, you encourage two desirable actions in the swing that will produce power and a right-to-left ball flight.

First, opening your stance slightly creates a little extra muscle tension along your left side during the backswing. This causes your hips to unwind with incredible speed on the downswing, giving you more power. Second, because your hips are unwinding so quickly on the downswing, your shoulders are left behind in a closed position as the clubhead approaches the ball. This helps you swing the club down from the inside, encouraging a draw.

Don't, however, set your stance more open than is demonstrated on page 78.

Monitor position of hands

Your grip isn't the only hands-related factor that can lead to a slice. Also important is the position of your hands in relation to the ball at address. Many slicers have their hands set even with the zipper on their trousers, which is too far behind the ball. Through impact, they are in a position completely different from what they were in at address. Their hands are now ahead of the ball instead of behind it, which has the effect of opening the clubface. Wham, another slice.

Position your hands forward at address so they are even with the crease on your left trouser pocket. By aligning your shoulders a little to the right, aim the club where you want the ball to *start,* in other words, open to your target. That's important. Don't fall into the trap of thinking that because you want the ball to fly from right to left the clubface should be closed at impact. It should be *closing*—not closed.

These adjustments shift the point at which the bottom of your swing occurs. In this case, back of where it would normally be. Your setup will encourage the club to swing back and later into the ball more from the inside. All of which gives your hands more time to release through the shot. And the more hand action you employ, the more right-to-left spin you impart on the ball.

Stick a club shaft in the ground about two feet outside your right foot and halfway between the target line and your stance line. Swing the club back outside the shaft.

Swing club along target line going back, then inside target line coming down

OK, now you're saying it's all very well to "encourage" the correct inside swing path with the position of your hands at address, but where *exactly* should the club go? There are two key positions that, when blended together, will produce the type of swing necessary to achieve a draw. To perfect them, get an old clubshaft and stick it in the ground about two feet outside your right foot and directly between your stance line and the target line. Without a ball at first, swing the clubhead back along the target line as far as practicable so it travels *outside* the clubshaft that is stuck in the ground *(p. 80)*.

Note how you have free, maximum extension with your left

...then inside it on the downswing.

arm. This will widen and lengthen your swing arc, making it easier to generate more clubhead speed.

On the downswing your club should pass *inside* the shaft stuck in the ground *(p. 81)*. To accomplish this, the club must lag behind you so that your hands are nearer to the target line than the clubhead. This insures that the clubhead approaches the ball from inside the line of play, which is the first step to helping you produce a draw.

Make your swing a "figure 8"

If you find that the previous drill still doesn't get the club inside the line on the downswing—and it's hard to go from one extreme to the other in a short space of time—here's a more exaggerated move you can try.

One reason a slice is so hard to cure is that your perspective of your own swing is warped. You may *feel* you're swinging along a draw-producing, inside-to-out swing path, when in fact you're cutting across the ball from outside to in. The solution to this is correct mental imagery, a conception of the correct swing path that translates easily into the real thing.

The best mental image to produce a draw is thinking of the swing as a figure 8. Lee Trevino used just such an image when, in search of more distance, he converted from his long-time fade to a draw.

First, note again the address position. The stance is slightly open, the feet aligned a little to the left of the target. Not only does that bring you the benefits outlined above, but it also helps prevent any overturning on the way back. Look at it this way. If you close your stance, or draw your right foot away from the target line, you run the risk of turning too far on the backswing. At the top, your body is pointed so far to the right that you'll instinctively come over the top, or spin your shoulders, in an effort to make the club travel down the target line on the down-swing (sound familiar?). With an open stance you'll sense the necessity of swinging the clubhead into the ball from the inside.

Next comes the takeaway, which is the most critical element of the figure-8 swing. **You must take the club back along a path parallel to your stance line.** After you reach the top of the backswing, start the downswing by letting your arms draw down and inward so your right arm falls closer to your right hip. This allows you to swing the club into the ball from the inside, completing the bottom half of the "8." After impact, the club swings out to the right of the target, further defining the "8." The club travels up and around at the finish, completing the figure 8.

The swing of most slicers resembles a figure 8, but they run the race backward. The club traces the figure 8 in the wrong direction. Instead of taking the club back parallel to the target line, they whip it back excessively to the inside trying, no doubt, to create that "in-to-out" path they've heard about. Right there they are dead, for once they reach the top, as we've said before, there is no place for their arms and shoulders to go but "over the top." They cast the club out across the target line so that the clubhead approaches the ball from outside the line of play. Result? Vicious slice.

Follow clubs on ground

Getting your club to make that figure 8 move is a major step in curing your slice. But it can sometimes be a hard move to ingrain. So make it easy for yourself with this drill *(p. 84)* devised by Scott Davenport. Place two clubs on the ground about six inches outside your line of play. The back club should be placed just behind the ball going away from the target and parallel to your toe line. This indicates the path you want your club to take at the start of your backswing. The front club should

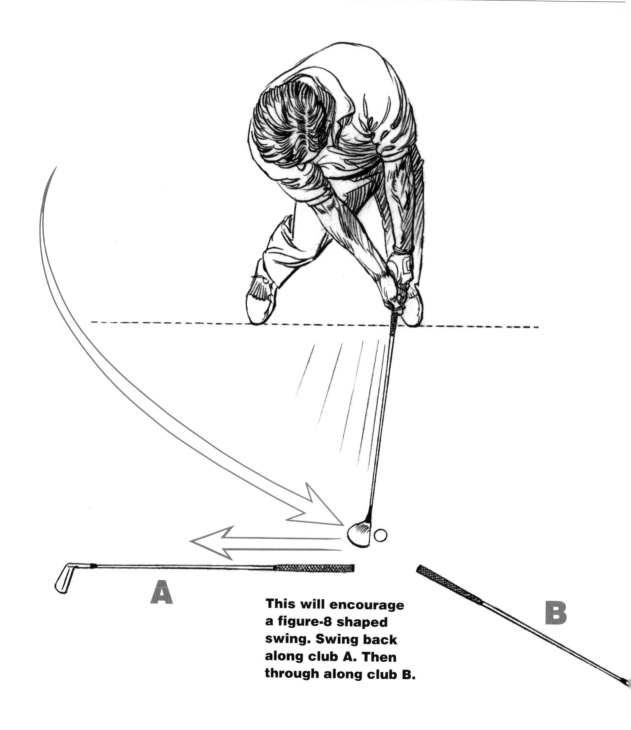

A

B

This will encourage a figure-8 shaped swing. Swing back along club A. Then through along club B.

be canted away from the ball, pointing to a spot about 15 yards to the right of your target. This indicates the path you want the club to follow on the forward swing.

Now practice swinging your club back along the back club and forward toward the front club.

Keep left knee flexed throughout swing

As we've said over and over, "coming over the top," or spinning the right shoulder toward the target line at the start of the downswing, is far and away the most common slicing cause. It occurs due to poor movement in an unlikely area: the left knee. When you slice it's an even-money bet that you straighten your left leg at the beginning of the downswing. This is disastrous according to Trevino. When you straighten your left leg, your right shoulder "follows" the left knee and, just like that, your shoulders are aligned to the left of the target. You can't help but cut across the ball on an outside-to-in path and slice.

To draw the ball, the left leg must remain flexed throughout the downswing, with the left knee driving steadily toward the target. See what happens when you keep your left leg flexed. Instead of your right shoulder spinning out, it works "down and under" your chin and keeps your upper body square to the target line.

As the left knee moves toward the target, you should have the definite sensation that it is closer to the target line than the right knee. If the left knee straightens and locks, it will feel like your left kneecap is moving back toward your heel.

If your legs work properly, your arms won't flail away from your body. By keeping your left leg flexed at the knee, your arms are actually drawn closer to your upper body and are transported into the ball along an inside path, which makes it possible to draw the ball.

You'll find it very difficult to come over the top if your left leg remains flexed. Only after impact should your left leg straighten.

All of the above tells you how your body and the club should be moving in a draw swing. But what about your hands and arms? **The importance of the roles played by your hands and wrists in the production of a draw cannot be overstated.** Not only do your hands have to be positioned exactly on the club and in relation to the ball, your wrists have to work properly in conjunction with the turning of your body.

Here's how Golf Digest Schools' Instructor Tom Ness teaches the correct motions:

1. Start without a club and go slowly at first. Your palms parallel and facing, swing your hands back letting your left wrist flatten and right wrist bend back. Swing through, maintaining the flat left wrist.

2. Next, grip down the shaft so that the clubhead is about a foot from your hands. This will give you great feedback on how the left wrist controls the clubface throughout the swing.

3. Finally, move on to making half swings with your hands on the grip, just as they would be normally. You don't need a ball. Keep your focus on your left wrist. As long as it is flat and vertical when your hands are about waist high both back and through, you're fine.

Keep shaft pointing at target line

This simple drill *(pp. 88-89)* will help your swing plane as well as your wrist's hinging motion. One of the most common causes of a slice is attempting to force the clubhead "down the target line" through impact. The clubshaft has to point "at" not "down" that line.

Tee a ball as shown, then make it the middle of a line of balls stretching toward and away from the target.

Now address the teed ball, but grip the club at the head end so the shaft is pointing at the ball. As you swing back, try to keep the shaft pointing at the line of balls. That will keep you on plane.

When you swing through your aim is the same: to keep your shaft pointing directly at the line of balls. See how you can do that and still have the club move to the inside? Don't make the slicer's common mistake and have the clubhead go "down the line." That only leaves the clubface open and forces your left wrist to look upward.

Logo looks up—back and through

Once the two previous drills have given you a feel for how your hands and wrists should be working, you're ready to hit some shots. Only short ones, though. You still want to focus more on your hands and their motion rather than the ball. One of the biggest problems you have to overcome is the "hit" impulse you had in your old swing, so stay focused on your hinge action. Don't anticipate impact.

Set up to a ball as if you are going to hit a short pitch shot. Notice how the company logo on the lower end of the grip is looking upward, not to the left or right (if your grip doesn't have a logo, put some tape on, or use a marker pen). That's vital. As you swing back, the logo should remain facing up. This happens only if your hands duplicate the motion of a swinging door.

The same is true at impact and on your followthrough. Keep that logo looking upward.

To stay on-plane, keep the shaft pointing at the line of balls, both back and through.

YES

YES

If you try to swing the clubhead "down the line," you'll leave the clubface open at impact.

NO

Here's how Golf Digest Schools' Instructor Tom Ness teaches the correct motions:

▌ Start without a club and go slowly at first. Your palms parallel and facing, swing your hands back letting your left wrist flatten and right wrist bend back. Swing through, maintaining the flat left wrist.

2 Next, grip down the shaft so that the clubhead is about a foot from your hands. This will give you great feedback on how the left wrist controls the clubface throughout the swing.

3 Finally, move on to making half swings with your hands on the grip, just as they would be normally. You don't need a ball. Keep your focus on your left wrist. As long as it is flat and vertical when your hands are about waist high both back and through, you're fine.

SOME EVEN STRONGER MEDICINE

If, even after working your way through all of the exercises detailed in this chapter, you are still having trouble getting the ball to move from right-to-left, or, heaven forbid, still slicing, try these hook-inducing drills:

Ball above feet flattens plane

Set up on a slope, the ball above your feet. That will flatten the plane of your swing and encourage the inside-to-inside arc the club must follow.

Now go ahead and hit some shots. Start slowly. Don't try to hit the ball hard at first. Focus on your hands and the clubface. Feel how your right hand works over your left, closing the clubface as it moves through impact and into the follow-through. Do that consistently and the ball will fly from right to left every time.

Split your grip

Using a short, lofted iron, separate your hands on the club, sliding the right hand down several inches to the bottom of the grip. Close your shoulders slightly and think of keeping them closed throughout the forward swing. You won't actually be able to do this, but the thought will make you swing the club out to the right of your target. At the same time the split grip lets you more easily rotate your hands and forearms and turn the clubface over.

Practice this motion without a ball, making sure you swing down from the inside to out while keeping your upper body back behind the ball. Then do the drill with a ball on a tee, as illustrated on the facing page, positioned about in the center of your stance. If you are doing it properly, you will get a snap hook, the ball starting to the right but quickly ducking left. As the motion becomes more familiar, gradually slide your hands together,

A split grip makes it easier for you to rotate your hands and forearms through impact.

ROLL OVER

eventually assuming your normal grip. Gradually move your setup back to normal, too, and as you do so move to a longer, less-lofted iron. Keep adjusting your rotation until you are getting a gentle little draw.

Toss a ball to learn the feel

Pick a target—a tree or other object—and set up as if you are going to strike a golf ball to it. Instead, toss a ball to the target with a sidearm/underhand motion, much the same as a baseball throw by a second baseman when he scoops up a grounder and makes a quick toss to first base *(p. 95).*

If at first you're throwing the ball high and left of the target, it's because you're swinging the right shoulder but not rotating the right hand. Let the arm swing and rotate the palm in a counterclockwise motion as you send the ball to the target. This will give you the same feeling you get when you swing a golf club from the inside of your target line with the arms and hands rotating to turn over the clubface.

Swing in chair to feel club turning

Sit on a chair and hold the club straight out in front of you at eye level, parallel to the ground. Then just swing your arms back and through, as in a normal swing. On the backswing, allow the right arm to fold and the left arm to swing over it. On the forward swing, the opposite happens—the left arm folds as the right arm crosses over after passing the impact position.

Because your upper body cannot move and get out in front of the ball, this Jim Flick drill *(pp. 96-97)* lets you identify the feeling of swinging from the inside and the feeling of your arms and the clubface turning and squaring as the club returns to its original position at impact. The back of the chair will keep your hips and shoulders from interfering, allowing your arms to control the swing. Do this exercise a number of times, then try to duplicate the feeling from a normal address position.

Tossing a ball like a second baseman helps you feel an in-to-out swing.

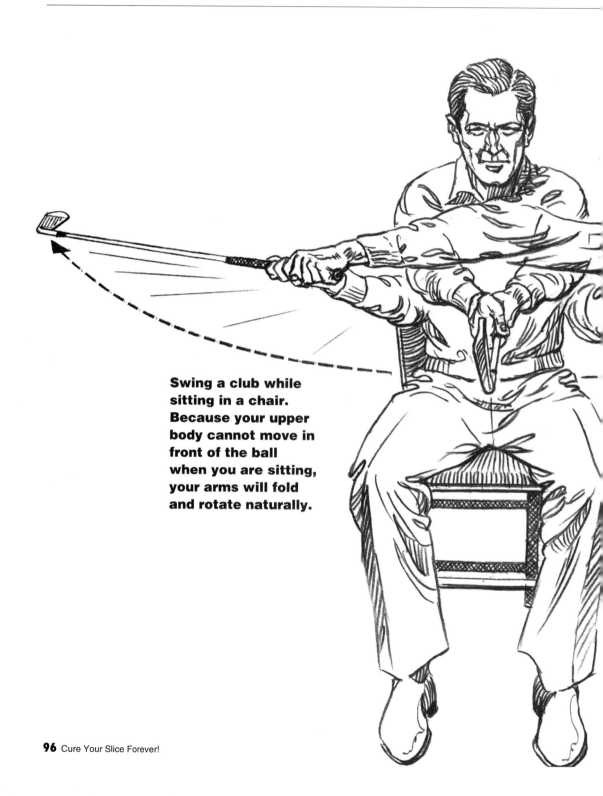

Swing a club while sitting in a chair. Because your upper body cannot move in front of the ball when you are sitting, your arms will fold and rotate naturally.

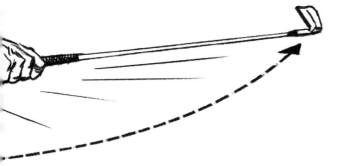

"Tempo is the ingredient that ties the swing together and produces the timing that is so essential to effective ball-striking."

AL GEIBERGER, TEMPO

5. Tempo

Now that your mechanics are more or less set, there is one final piece to fit into your golfing jigsaw.

Tempo.

Tempo is the timing, the pace of your swing. Not just during a single shot, but throughout an entire round. It's your personal pace on the golf course, too: Walking to the shot, setting up to hit it and making your swing. Good tempo is especially crucial on the tee where so many slicers get tense and revert back to their old, out-to-in swings.

Think about it: How many times have you seen a sweet-swinging slicer? Not often. One of the first things you notice about slicers is the abruptness of their actions. When you hit a slice you create speed, sure. But usually at the wrong times. There is certainly no sensation of "easiness" about the backswing, or smoothness about the transition from back to downswing, or gradual acceleration through impact, all the way to a balanced finish.

Slicers belong more to the school of hurried backswings, rushed transitions and early releases. By the time the club gets to the ball it is actually slowing down. Add that to the fact that an early, "over the top" move steepens the downswing, and the potential for long straight shots is all but dissipated.

The saddest aspect of all this is that **every golfer, slicer or not, would improve with better tempo.** Without even touching their mechanics, everyone could hit better shots simply by staying in balance and accelerating the clubhead through impact.

Be clear, however. We're not just talking about that hoary cliché, "swinging slower" here. After all, if you take a bad, fast swing and slow it down what do you have left? A bad slow swing. Having said that, what is true is that a bad, rhythmic swing is markedly better than an out-of-sync bad swing.

Good tempo is that important. It may be the most underrated part of any golf swing. You hear a lot about the importance of the fundamentals we've already covered in previous chapters—grip, stance, ball position—but not nearly enough is said about tempo. Which is surprising. No matter how good your fundamentals are, poor tempo almost always leads to poor results. Especially under pressure, more shots are ruined by loss of rhythm than for any other reason.

And, as we've already touched on, a slow swing is not necessarily good and a fast swing bad. What is a good tempo for one player may not be for another. There have always been great players at either end of the tempo spectrum. The secret is that all of them, whether relatively fast or slow, make *smooth* swings. They may be made at different speeds, but there is never anything jerky about them. From address, they accelerate smoothly and gradually all the way to impact.

So what you must do is find your own natural rhythm. If you walk fast, chew fast and talk fast, then chances are your swing is going to follow that lead. Similarly, if you are a more laid-back individual, then your action is going to be a bit slower.

Neither, of course, is bad. You just have to stick to what is right for you.

Once you have made that discovery or decision, don't make the mistake of trying to change it. Particularly in the middle of a round. Be what you are as far as swinging the club goes. Just try to swing every club—from driver to wedge—at the same pace. The following exercises and drills will help you do just that.

Before you start: Work on your waggle

There is no way you can make a consistently smooth, rhythmic backswing—at any tempo—if your muscles are tight and tense. Just moving the club to and fro before you start back keeps you relaxed at address. Make it rhythmic, too. Counting "1-2" to yourself as the club goes back and forward is a good prelude to a smooth swing. But the great thing is you can basically do whatever you want, as long as you develop your own waggle until it is ingrained into your preshot routine.

Going back: Focus again on your shoulder turn

Although you've already seen the benefits a full and proper shoulder turn can bring to your swing, it can help your tempo, too. Bad tempo often results from mentally over-complicating your swing mechanics. Simplify things. Concentrate on your shoulder turn. Swing at half speed. Get all your moving parts synchronized.

By making the good turn we described in Chapter 3, you ensure that there is no possibility of swaying onto the outside of your right foot. Your weight must remain centered on the inside/middle portion of your foot.

Try to feel as if your left shoulder is under your chin at the top (*p. 102*). When you achieve that, you know you have made a full shoulder turn. In front of a full-length mirror, make some

Try to feel as if your left shoulder is under your chin at the top.

backswings at half speed focusing on these important check-points.

From the top: Make a smooth transition

We mentioned balance earlier. It is a crucial part of any good swing. Lose your balance and you stand a good chance of losing your ball, too.

The area of your swing where balance is most important is in the transition—the point where backswing becomes downswing. If you are still hitting that infernal slice, ask yourself: Am I making a smooth transition? If you're not, it can usually be traced back to your initial move away from the ball. It has to be *smooth*. Not ponderous and certainly not rushed. **Use your backswing to establish the momentum of your swing.** Smooth acceleration is your aim. That will give you time to avoid that dreaded "over the top" move and make the proper pulling motion on the way down. Get it right and you'll finish nicely on your left side.

If, however, you start back too slowly you have to compensate by speeding up excessively later; too fast and it is difficult to maintain control. Both lead to a lack of synchronization between club and body at the start of the downswing. Either the club outruns the body or the body outruns the club. The inevitable result is an off-balance finish and a poor shot. In your case, another slice.

Impact: Only one fast moment

If you are going to remember one tempo key as you swing, make it this one: **swing as fast as you can while still maintaining control of both your body and the club.** And make the fastest point in your swing the impact area. Not going back. Not from the top. At the ball is where you want the clubhead to be

**Make impact your
"fast moment."
Accelerate the
clubhead into
the ball.**

moving as fast as it can go.

This is important. You can't have more than one fast spot in your swing. You can't swing fast twice. Try it and see; it can't be done. So you must start the club back smoothly, start it down leisurely and save that one fast moment for impact. At all times your muscles must be relaxed and supple. A thought that will help you accomplish this is, "swing easy." How many times have you told yourself that and proceeded to hit the ball 20 yards farther than normal? If your muscles are loose and relaxed, they can swing the club faster than if they are tight. Not only will you hit the ball farther, but you'll be more accurate as well.

Look at the illustration on the opposite page. The player's hands and arms are adding momentum and will arrive at their maximum speed at the moment club meets ball. If you sense your "fast moment" is happening too soon—and if you've been slicing it almost certainly has been—feel as if you are striking the ball "before" the club reaches maximum speed. That way, the clubhead will at least still be accelerating—not slowing down—at impact.

The whole swing: Lift, turn, swing down

If the feelings described in the previous drills prove elusive, try this exercise (pp. 106-107). Stand in your normal address position, lift the club straight up in front of your face and cock your wrists. Make the shoulder turn you have been working so diligently on. That should put you in the perfect top-of-the-backswing position. Now swing down and through the ball. Obviously you won't be able to generate a whole lot of clubhead speed, but with practice you'll be surprised at how well and how far you can strike the ball.

When you can smack the ball out there pretty good, try to transfer the feeling this drill gives you of being "behind" the ball

Smooth your tempo. From address...

Lift the club straight up...

**Turn your
shoulders...**

**Swing down
and through.**

at the top to real shots. Hit maybe three shots, then go back to the drill. Gradually build up the number of "real" shots as the feeling becomes more ingrained.

Practice with feet together

This is a simple drill *(p. 109)*, but very effective. Take your new, square to the target stance, then move your feet together until they are almost touching. Hit some shots.

You will soon learn that only smooth backswings allow you to make decent contact with the ball. If you can stay centered and make a proper turn around your central axis (your spine), then your tempo is probably pretty good. If you swing too fast, however, that central axis will shift to the right and you will fall over.

Either way, you get instant feedback on both the tempo and balance of your backswing.

Hit three-quarter shots

If you're working on your tempo never try to hit the ball hard. All that does is quicken your swing and make a slice more likely. Instead, hit three-quarter shots. That doesn't mean making a shorter swing or less of a turn, though. It is merely a slower delivery of the clubhead through the ball. The only major difference is that you should grip down on the club a little. That reduces the width of your arc and therefore the power you can generate.

With, say, a 5-iron, hit shots imagining you are making practice swings without a ball. In other words, relax. That is a good feeling to foster.

Don't worry too much about where the ball is going at first. Focusing on the quality of your shots only takes your mind off your swing. And that leads to more tension. So concentrate on

With your feet almost touching, swing back. Only if you are well-balanced will you stay upright.

making a smooth, flowing swing, merely letting the ball get in the way of the clubhead. Anything to rid yourself of the "hit" instinct which previously led to so many of those slices.

Some quick tempo tips

Sometimes all you need to make a smooth swing is one simple swing thought. Try one, or some, or even all of these tips (not at once of course!). You never know.

Just don't make the mistake of taking them too literally. These are feelings, not hard and fast mechanical laws. So treat them as such.

1. Lighten your grip so that you can better feel the clubhead.
2. Initiate your backswing with your body and shoulders. They are easier to control than your hands.
3. Let your body and club work at the same speed. Start them back together and down together.
4. Narrow your stance and try to make longer swings. That helps your balance, too.
5. Lift your club half an inch off the ground at address. That helps eliminate tension.
6. Hit balls wearing tennis shoes. You have to swing smoothly to maintain your balance.
7. Make your full swing like a putt. Count 1-2 on your back and through swings.
8. Practice making full swings at half speed.
9. Start slow and easy, then try to speed up gradually.
10. Do all your practice with a wedge. It's easier to feel your tempo when the club is moving slowly.

And finally.... Don't drink too much coffee in the mornings!!

"Great players are great planners. A sound game plan is essential in golf."

JOHNNY MILLER, PURE GOLF.

6. And if nothing works... How to play with your slice

As should be obvious to you by now, slicing is a serious business. But, according to Peter Kostis, it isn't terminal. Contrary to what people say, you *can* play with a slice. You do have to perform under certain constraints—there are obvious limitations on what you can and cannot do with the ball—but it is still possible to make the best of what you have at your disposal.

Don't get the wrong impression, though. If you are still a chronic slicer continue to work on the things outlined in the previous chapters; take some lessons and work toward straightening out your ball flight. Within that process, however, you still have to play. Here are some of the more difficult problems posed to slicers on the course, with some tips on how to make the best of each situation.

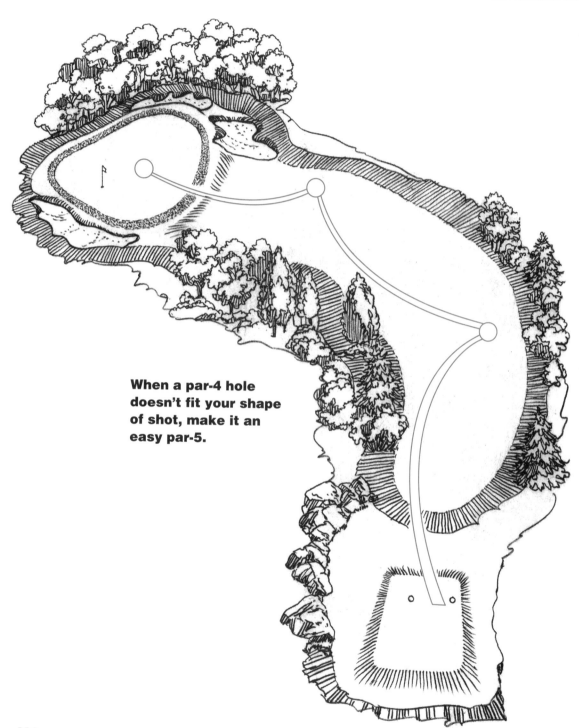

When a par-4 hole doesn't fit your shape of shot, make it an easy par-5.

Right-to-left dogleg:
Rely on your short game

Your problem is getting comfortable. It is difficult to feel "right" when the hole doesn't suit your ball flight. And that feeling can translate into tension, which makes the problem even worse. To get by the difficulty such a par-4 presents, you need a plan. Don't mess with the dogleg. Play the hole the long way round. Play it down the right-hand side as a three-shot par 5.

Tee off with a club you can slice safely into the right side of the fairway. Because the hole is going left, that means using less club. Take, say, your 3-wood. Your next step—and this is crucial—is to lay up to a point that gives you a comfortable shot into the green. Even if the green is reachable with an exceptional shot, don't get greedy and go for it. More times than not, your ball will roll into a sand trap in front of the green. And that leaves you with a difficult long bunker shot.

So, if you know you can hit your wedge 95 yards, hit your second shot with a club that will leave you 95 yards from the hole. Your third shot should then be reasonably straightforward. Hit it close and the worst you can make is 5—and sometimes you'll make a 4. In other words, play the hole for a 5 with the possibility of making a 4. Don't get overambitious, gamble for a 4 and end up making a 7 or 8.

Clearly, making this plan work depends a great deal on your ability to hit that third shot. **Practice your short irons until you know how far you can hit each one.** If you're going to rely on your short game, you'd better know it.

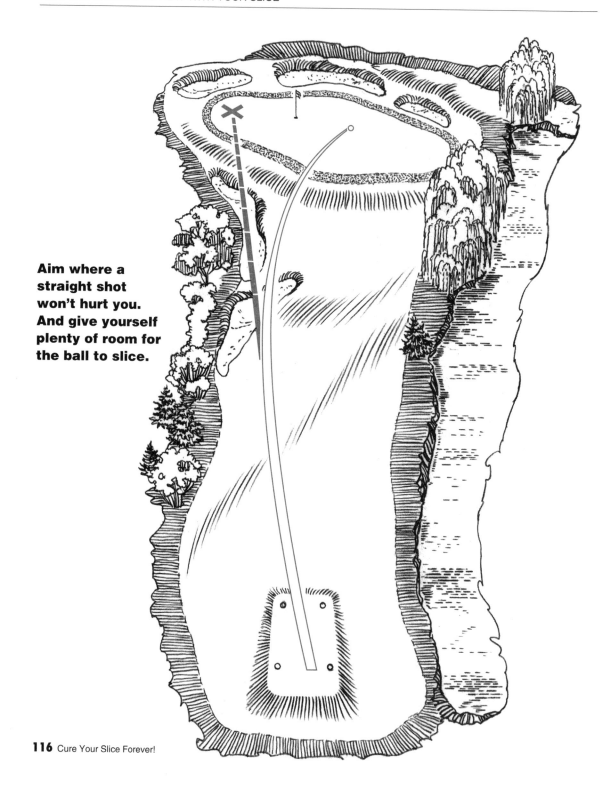

Aim where a straight shot won't hurt you. And give yourself plenty of room for the ball to slice.

Trouble short or right:
Swing in balance

One of the biggest fears for a slicer is out-of-bounds, water, bunkers or trees down the right. They all create tension because your ball is curving toward them.

The solution, as you might expect, is to aim far enough left to allow for your slice. On the tee take advantage of the full width of the fairway by teeing up as far on the right as you can, aiming away from the trouble. Let your slice curve the ball back.

Wherever you are, though, swing in balance. A lot of slicers, as we've already said in Chapter 1, get into trouble when, in an effort to twist to the left and stop the ball going to the right, they lift their spine angle coming forward. That lays the club even more open than usual, the ball flies miles right and, inevitably, short of the target. Thus, these guidelines are equally applicable when the trouble is in front of you.

You must trust your aim and your swing. Aim as far left as you safely can and maintain your spine angle throughout your swing. But, again, **don't aim where a straight shot will hurt you.** After all, even the worst slicer can hit one straight now and again.

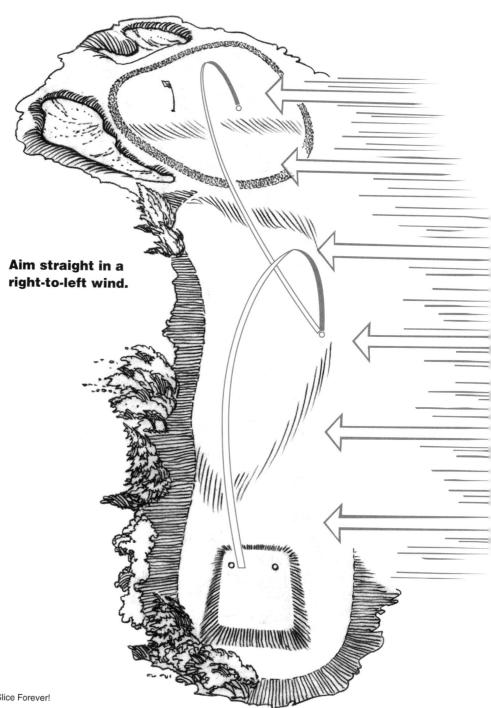

**Aim straight in a
right-to-left wind.**

In the wind:
Make preswing adjustments

Downwind: Everyone loves to play downwind and slicers are no exception. Understand only that the ball will not curve as much, so don't aim where a straight shot will hurt you. Don't aim at those bunkers on the left anticipating that the ball will fade back. Aim just inside any left-side trouble.

Left-to-right: The ball will go farther and curve more than normal. Your slice will ride the wind, so remember to make your club selection and adjust your aim accordingly.

Right-to-left/Headwind: Either of these factors pose particular problems for slicers. A slice tends to climb so a headwind will influence the ball more. And a right-to-left wind is, in effect, a headwind for a slicer, so the result is the same.

Your keys here are all preswing. Make three adjustments: Take more club, stand closer to the ball and move the ball back in your stance (to position A). By taking more club you compensate somewhat for the the loss of distance the wind causes. Standing closer and moving the ball back will cause the shot to fly lower.

These adjustments hold true for both right-to-left winds and headwinds. The only difference is that in a right-to-left wind you need to aim almost straight at your target rather than to the left. The wind will negate a good deal of your left-to-right spin.

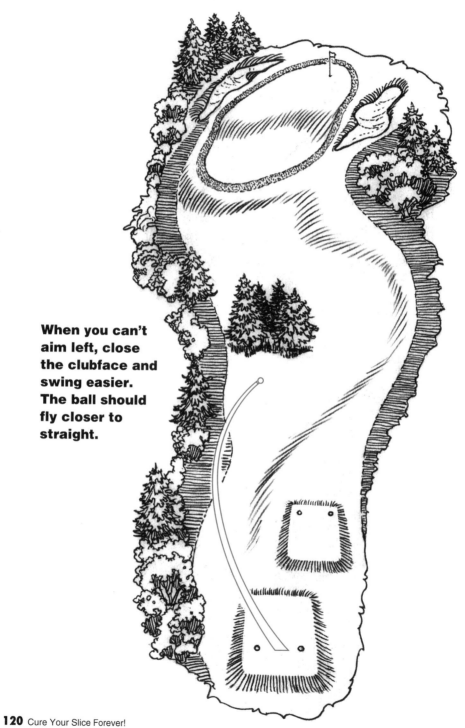

When you can't aim left, close the clubface and swing easier. The ball should fly closer to straight.

Can't aim left?
Use more loft

This is every slicer's nightmare. What do you do when a tree or some other obstruction prevents you from starting the ball left? You need to replace starting direction as an adjustment. There are a few options:

1. Preset the club in a closed position. Then, assuming you make your normal swing, the ball will fly straight. This sounds simple, but isn't. Practice it until you can be reasonably sure of yourself on the course.

2. Use a more lofted club. Loft creates more backspin than sidespin so the ball will fly straighter.

3. Swing easier. That also helps eliminate sidespin and therefore curvature on the ball.

4. Chip out, take your punishment and move on. If you are in any doubt, use this last resort.

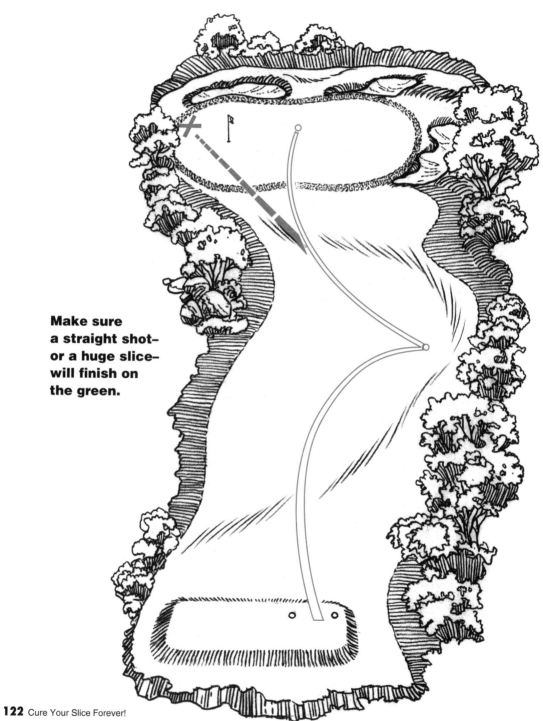

**Make sure
a straight shot–
or a huge slice–
will finish on
the green.**

Pin on left:
Aim inside edge of green

The golden rule here: **Always aim inside the green's perimeter.** Don't aim any farther left than the edge of the green. That gives you the whole width of the green in which to accommodate your slice, and even a straight shot will finish on the putting surface.

This may seem a little defensive in that you are basically playing away from the flag, your slice finishing on the right side of the green, but that way the percentages are in your favor. The last thing you want to do is miss to the left. You'll leave yourself a difficult chip or pitch with little green to work with. Double bogey is possible from such a place. Better to be on the green with a good chance of par or, at worst, a three-putt bogey.

Following these guidelines means that you are going to have your fair share of lengthy putts. So practice your lag putting and short putting. It is like the lay up to 95 yards; if you're going to rely on your short game, you'd better have a good idea of your capabilities.

And a last resort....

Because slicing is a golfing disease that seems to feed on itself, sometimes drastic measures are needed to fight it. This is for those of you who are tired of hitting more and more weak shots to the right; tired of aiming farther and farther left to allow for your open clubface and out-to-in swingpath; and don't have the time or inclination to fix your slice properly.

If you've read all of this book you'll know that if you really want to kill your slice you need to square up your stance and work on turning so that you can swing the club into the ball from the inside. That, of course, is the right way to go. But it can take time and—let's be realistic—there are some of you who will find it difficult—if not impossible—to accomplish.

If all else fails, here's a (temporary) last resort to offset your slice. Aim right, close the clubface, then pull the ball to the target.

Try this instead *(pp. 124-125)*: take your normal stance, but aim to the right. Toe the club in, too. Now make your regular swing, focusing on releasing your right arm and the clubhead early, from the top of your swing. Feel as if you are throwing the head off the shaft.

Combine this swinging of the clubhead with the closed stance and clubface introduced at address, and you'll hit more solid shots that move left. In effect, you'll pull the ball on line. (OK, it's cheating, but sometimes a slicer's gotta do what a slicer's gotta do).

Don't play more than a couple of rounds this way. You don't want to ingrain the feeling of your over-the-top, pulling motion. Go back to Chapter 3 as soon as possible and work on your turn. Then work on "drawing" the ball in Chapter 4. You *can* learn to cure your slice forever!

JOHN HUGGAN a former senior editor in charge of instruction for Golf Digest, is now a contributing editor for the magazine. He has authored scores of articles with most of the world's top players and teachers. He also collaborated with David Leadbetter on his bestselling volumes, *The Golf Swing* and *Faults and Fixes*.

Huggan lives in Dunbar, Scotland with his wife and family. He writes regularly, covering golf for *The Herald*, Scotland's largest newspaper.